Instant Expert: **The Bible**

INSTANT EXPERT

THE BIBLE

→ Nick Page

LION

Published by Lion Books
an imprint of
Lion Hudson plc
Wilkinson House, Jordan Hill Road,
Oxford OX2 8DR, England
www.lionhudson.com/lion

ISBN 978 0 7459 5575 9
e-ISBN 978 0 7459 5783 8

First edition 2013

Acknowledgments
Scripture quotations taken from the Holy Bible, New
International Version, copyright © 1973, 1978, 1984
International Bible Society. Used by permission of Hodder
& Stoughton, a member of the Hodder Headline Group. All
rights reserved. "NIV" is a trademark of International Bible
Society. UK trademark number 1448790.

A catalogue record for this book is available from the British
Library

Printed and bound in the UK, February 2013, LH26

Contents

Introduction

The Bible: it's the most famous book in the world.

It's the most published book. No one knows how many Bibles have been published – the number is in the billions.

It's the most influential book. Whatever you think about it, it's one of the cornerstones of Western civilization. It has had a massive effect on language, culture, laws, art, and society. This book has changed the world.

It's the most widely read book. Every day, every week, millions of people read this book. They hear it read in church. They read it in the privacy of their own homes.

It's the most smuggled book. Many countries around the world ban the Bible, and the Christians in those countries go to enormous lengths to get hold of a copy.

Let's face it: **it's the most important book in history**.

Given all of that, you'd think that reading the Bible is something that everyone should do. But there are some problems...

- **It's big.** This is one big book. It rolls in at around 750,000 words and is divided into sixty-six books, written by at least forty authors.

- **It's weird.** Often the version of the Bible that we are presented with is in a strange, old language. This is because people read from the King James Version, which was created in 1611. But even in modern versions there are strange terms: "covenant", "tabernacle", "Pharisee", and "ark", to name a few. Often, our response to reading a passage of the Bible is "Huh?"

- **It's boring.** Sometimes the Bible can seem incredibly dull. There are passages that give us the dimensions of buildings, detailed descriptions of ancient religious ritual, complicated family trees, and lists of tribes and clans which read like some kind of ancient telephone directory. Boring or what?

- **It's irrelevant.** It's all about people who died a long time ago and lived far, far away. They dressed in robes and herded sheep. They had names like Mephibosheth and Nebuchadnezzar. What have their lives got to do with today's world?

Those are all common objections. And they do have some truth to them. But let's have a very quick look at them, one by one.

- **The bigness thing.** Yes, it's big. But it was written by many different authors across a period of 1,500 years. It's about life, death, and everything between. You'd expect more than thirty-two pages and a few cartoons. Anyway, you don't have to read it all at once. We can read as little, or as much, as we like.

- **The weirdness thing.** You don't have to read the King James Version! There are many modern translations available. There are, admittedly, some specific biblical terms but not that many. And while there are, undoubtedly, things in the Bible that are difficult to understand and many passages that are open to different interpretations, the vast majority of the Bible is straightforward.

- **The boring thing.** It's true that there are things that won't thrill us. But for every boring bit there are tons of exciting bits. Yes, you get long family trees (which some cultures find exciting – even though they might not be our kind of "thing"), but you also get songs, drama, stories, sword fights, love poetry, evil villains, virtuous heroes, surprise twists, and prophets wandering around in their underwear (among other things).

And that leads me to...

- **The irrelevance thing.** One of the myths about the Bible is that because it was written so long ago, it can't have anything to say to us. But the people in the Bible are in many ways just like us. Of course they dress differently and act in some strange and unusual ways, but the fundamental issues they wrestle with face us all. The Bible talks about love, peace, war, happiness, freedom, greed, forgiveness, sex, possessions, truth … and a whole lot more. All just as relevant today.

All of this is why the Bible is still the world's most published book. Despite the perceived difficulties it still exerts a massive influence on our world.

In which case, it's not a bad idea to get a sense of where the Bible came from, how people use it, and what it's all about.

That's where this book comes in.

This book will help you get an overall understanding of the Bible – what it is, where it came from, what happens in it.

- Chapter 1: *What is the Bible?* gives a brief overview of the Bible and a guide to finding your way around.

- Chapter 2: *What happens in the Bible?* gives an outline of the overall biblical story.

- Chapter 3: *Who wrote the Bible?* looks at issues of authorship and composition.

- Chapter 4: *Who put the Bible together?* explores how the Bible was compiled and who decided the final contents.

- Chapter 5: *The Bible: book by book* tells you more about the various Bible books.

- Chapter 6: *How do we read the Bible?* describes some tools and resources to help you explore the Bible for yourself.

The Bible isn't just for the devout. It was never meant as something that only the holy few could read. It's meant for everyone. And for centuries ordinary people of all creeds and backgrounds have read the Bible for themselves.

So I hope this book will encourage you to give it a go. You never know what you'll find!

1. What is the Bible?

Let's start with the name: the Bible.

It's really a made-up word, an English-language spelling of the Greek words *ta biblia*, which mean, "the books".

It's a reminder that the Bible is not *a* book, but a collection of books: sixty-six books bound into one volume. It's a one-volume library, containing many different types of writing: poetry, history, laws, prophecy, proverbs and sayings, stories, letters, and more.

The holy books

The first person to use *ta biblia* to describe the scriptures was Clement of Alexandria, writing around AD 215. He was talking about the Hebrew scriptures – the Christian "Old Testament". It was his pupil, Origen, who used "the books" to describe *all* the scriptures – including the Christian ones – in AD 223. But for centuries people didn't call this collection "the Bible". Jerome, writing in the fourth century, used the term *bibliotheca*, which means "library" or "collection of books", and this was the common term used for centuries among Latin speakers.

This collection of books is grouped into two sections:

- The Hebrew scriptures or Old Testament (thirty-nine books)
- The Christian scriptures or New Testament (twenty-seven books)

Some Bibles also have some extra material which is known as the Apocrypha. These books appear in Bibles used by the Catholic and Orthodox churches, but most Protestant Bibles omit them.

The Hebrew scriptures or Old Testament

The first part of the Bible contains the sacred writings of Judaism, written from around 1400 BC to 400 BC.

Christians call this section the Old Testament, but the Jewish name is the Tanakh. In the Jewish "Bible" the individual books are organized into three sections: Torah (the Law), Nevi'im (the Prophets) and Ketuvim (the Writings). The first letters of each section – TNK – give the acronym Tanakh.

The Christian Old Testament contains the same books, but arranged differently. (In Christian Bibles the books are arranged into the Law, Histories, Wisdom, and Major and Minor Prophets.)

Since the action of the Old Testament covers a period of many thousands of years, dating the composition is difficult. The oldest parts of the Old Testament were probably written around 1100 BC, although they describe events that took place many centuries earlier.

The Old Testament is written almost entirely in Hebrew, but it does contain some small parts in a different language – Aramaic. This language was spoken in the region after the Jews returned from their exile in Babylon in the sixth century BC. Although Hebrew remained the language of their religion, the people of Jesus' time spoke Aramaic.

Torah

The first five books of the Bible – Genesis to Deuteronomy – are known by several names. The Jewish name is Torah, which means "Instruction", but you might also hear them called "the Pentateuch", "the Law" or "the Books of Moses". These books contain the core material of Judaism. As well as tales of Jewish ancestors, the Torah contains the Jewish religious, legal, and ethical code. According to rabbinic tradition these are contained in 613 *mitzvot*, or commandments: 365 restrictions and 248 positive commands. In synagogues, the Torah is read from a Sefer Torah, or Torah scroll, a specially prepared parchment scroll written by a trained scribe.

The New Testament

The second section of the Bible is called the New Testament. This is the collection of Christian scriptures. These writings fall into three main groups: Gospels and Acts; letters from early church leaders such as Paul, Peter, and John; and Revelation, which was probably sent as a letter, but which, with its visionary, apocalyptic language, stands alone.

Unlike the Old Testament, the books of the New Testament were written over a short period of time, between around AD 50 and AD 90.

Testament

Testament means "promise". For Christians the "Old Testament" is the promise given by God to the Jews; the "New Testament" is the promise given through Jesus. This word was first used by Christians to describe the Tanakh around the end of the second century AD.

The New Testament was originally written in Greek. Jesus and his disciples spoke Aramaic – and some of their original words remain in the New Testament. But the New Testament was written for a wider audience: for Gentiles (the non-Jewish inhabitants of the Roman empire), and, since the time of Alexander the Great, the common language of the Mediterranean region was Greek. The type of Greek they spoke – found in the New Testament – has since been called *koine*, or common Greek. This was the everyday language of ordinary working people: traders, housewives, and shopkeepers.

As well as bits of Aramaic, there are also a few Latin words in the New Testament, but these are mainly technical and military terms such as centurion, *denarius* (the Roman coinage), and *mille* (the Roman mile). They remind us that Jesus lived in a land under military occupation.

The Apocrypha
Some Bibles also include a section known as the Apocrypha. These books are found in the Bibles of the Catholic and Eastern churches – but not in Jewish or modern Protestant Bibles. These books were mainly written in Greek and they come from the "gap years" between the end of the Old Testament and the beginning of the New, when Greek rulers sought to impose Greek culture onto the Jews. The Catholic and Eastern churches view these writings as authoritative, but at a lower level than the other books of the Hebrew scriptures.

Finding your way around
The books of the Bible are not organized alphabetically, but in collections of different types. In the Christian Bible they are grouped as follows:

THE TANAKH Hebrew Scriptures/ Old Testament	THE OLD TESTAMENT In Protestant Bibles	THE NEW TESTAMENT Christian Scriptures
TORAH **The Law** *Genesis, Exodus, Leviticus, Numbers, Deuteronomy*	**PENTATEUCH** **The Law** *Genesis, Exodus, Leviticus, Numbers, Deuteronomy*	**GOSPELS AND ACTS** *Matthew, Mark, Luke, John, Acts*
NEVI'IM **The Prophets** **FORMER PROPHETS** *Joshua, Judges, Samuel, Kings* **LATER PROPHETS** *Isaiah, Jeremiah, Ezekiel The Minor Prophets (Hosea, Joel, Amos, Obadiah, Jonah, Micah, Nahum, Habakkuk, Zephaniah, Haggai, Zechariah, Malachi)*	**HISTORIES** *Joshua, Judges, Ruth, Samuel, Kings, Chronicles, Ezra, Nehemiah, Esther* **WISDOM** *Job, Psalms, Proverbs, Ecclesiastes, Song of Songs*	**LETTERS** **PAUL'S LETTERS** *Romans, 1&2 Corinthians, Galatians, Ephesians, Philippians, Colossians, 1&2 Thessalonians, 1&2 Timothy, Titus, Philemon* **GENERAL OR "CATHOLIC" LETTERS** *Hebrews, James, 1&2 Peter, 1,2&3 John, Jude*
KETUVIM **The Writings** **WRITINGS** *Psalms, Proverbs, Job, Song of Songs, Ruth, Lamentations, Ecclesiastes, Esther, Daniel, Ezra/Nehemiah, Chronicles*	**PROPHETS** **MAJOR PROPHETS** *Isaiah, Jeremiah, Lamentations, Ezekiel, Daniel* **MINOR PROPHETS** *Hosea, Joel, Amos, Obadiah, Jonah, Micah, Nahum, Habakkuk, Zephaniah, Haggai, Zechariah, Malachi*	**REVELATION** *The Revelation of John*

Each book of the Bible is subdivided into chapters and verses. These are useful for referring to specific parts of the Bible and for finding your way around. But we should remember that these were added much later. The chapter numbering system we use today dates from the thirteenth century, and the verse subdivisions date from the sixteenth century.

2. What happens in the Bible?

Although the Bible consists of many different books, it is, above all, a story. There is a narrative that threads through it. And it goes, broadly, like this...

In the beginning...
In the beginning, God creates the heavens and the earth. He fills the earth with plants and creatures. He looks at it and sees that it is good. He creates man and woman – Adam and Eve – and gives them a garden in a place called Eden, and the responsibility to look after it. They are given only one rule: don't eat the fruit of the tree in the middle of the garden. However, Eve is persuaded by a serpent to eat the fruit; she in turn persuades Adam. They have been tempted and have disobeyed God. The result is that they're thrown out of the garden and God's creation is no longer "good". This is the event known as **the fall**.

Noah and the flood
In the generations following the fall of Adam and Eve, both bad and good things enter the world. Humans start to farm the land and keep livestock, play music, and make tools. But evil also spreads through the world. Cain (Adam's eldest son) murders his brother Abel in a

fit of jealous rage. Things get so bad that God decides
to send a flood to destroy all humans. Only one family
is saved. Noah is a good man and he is commanded
to build an "ark", a huge floating box in which he, his
family, and a "breeding stock" of animals can ride
out the flood. Noah builds the ark, and when the flood
subsides, God promises that never again will he wipe
out humanity in this way. As a sign of this promise he
sends a rainbow. (Evil has not gone away, however. The
people try to build a tower to reach the heavens, and
God confounds them by confusing their languages.)

After this, God takes a new approach. He tells a man
called Abraham to move to the land of Canaan. God
promises that Abraham's descendants will be a great
nation – they will inhabit this land, and all of humanity
will be blessed by them. The promise made to Abraham
(and reaffirmed to others) is known as the **covenant**.

The patriarchs

Abraham, Isaac, and Jacob are known as the patriarchs
– the "fathers" of the Israelites. Abraham is very old
– in his nineties. But God keeps his promises and
Abraham's wife Sarah gives birth to Isaac. Isaac is
the father to twins, Esau and Jacob. (The covenant
is repeated several times to Abraham, as well as to
Abraham's son Isaac and his grandson Jacob. Among
the stipulations of the covenant is the instruction
that all male Jews should be circumcised.) Jacob is
a trickster who has to be "overcome" by God. God
changes Jacob's name to **Israel**, and henceforth the

people are known by this name. Jacob has twelve
children. Joseph – Jacob's favourite son – is unpopular
with his brothers. Enraged by his arrogance, they get
rid of him, by faking his death and selling him to slave
traders. Years later there is a famine in Canaan and
Jacob's sons go to Egypt to find food. They discover
that Joseph has survived and is now second in
command to the Pharaoh. Joseph invites the rest of his
family down to Egypt, so the entire clan moves there.

This takes us to the end of Genesis.

The exodus

In Egypt, the descendants of "Israel" multiply. (They
are now in twelve tribes, each tribal name taken
from one of Jacob's sons or grandsons.) Abraham's
descendants have, indeed, become a nation. But they
are a nation of slaves.

So God calls Moses, a man born a Hebrew slave
but raised an Egyptian prince. Moses kills a slave
driver and has to flee. In the desert he encounters
God in the form of a burning bush. Moses asks God
his name; God replies simply, "I am." Moses returns to
Egypt and commands the king to free the Israelites.
Pharaoh refuses, so God inflicts a series of plagues on
Egypt, culminating in the death of the first-born males
– human and livestock. After this, Pharaoh releases the
Israelites. God commands the Israelites to remember
this rescue in an annual festival, **the Passover**.

Moses leads the people to Mount Sinai, where God
gives them commandments and detailed instructions

on how they should live and how they should worship their God. These laws are written on stone tablets and put in a box. This is **the ark of the covenant**.

The people often rebel. They create false gods to worship. And when they get to the borders of Canaan, they are too scared to cross into the land. God punishes this lack of faith by making them wander in the desert for forty years. This is the **wandering in the wilderness**.

Eventually they return to the border of Canaan. Moses dies on a mountain overlooking the land. He hands over leadership to Joshua, who leads the Israelites into the land.

This story is contained in Exodus, Leviticus, Numbers, and Deuteronomy – the remaining four books of the Torah.

Conquest

At first the conquest goes well. But although the Israelites settle the land, some of the old Canaanite inhabitants remain with their own ways of worship. After Joshua's death, society descends into chaos. The pattern repeats itself: Israel turns away from God; God raises up a foreign nation to punish them; the people cry out to God to save them; and God raises up a hero – a "judge" – to rescue them. Then the people turn away from God, and the whole cycle starts again. The judges – leaders such as Deborah, Gideon, and Samson – bring only occasional light into the darkness.

This story is told in Joshua and Judges. Ruth, also, is set in the time of the judges.

Kings

After the chaos depicted in Judges, the people demand a king. Although not exactly enthusiastic about the idea, God agrees. The first choice, Saul, is a failure. So God selects David, a young shepherd, to be next. After Saul's death, David becomes king, fighting a series of successful campaigns and making Jerusalem his capital. But David commits adultery and murder, and the rest of his reign is full of tragedy and conflict. Still God promises that someone from David's family line will always be on Israel's throne. David is succeeded by Solomon, who builds a magnificent temple. This is the origin of **the Temple in Jerusalem**. But in the end, Solomon turns away from God

This story is told in 1 and 2 Samuel and in 1 and 2 Chronicles. Many of the psalms are attributed to David and reflect on episodes in his life, while the traditional account credits Solomon with writing Ecclesiastes, Song of Songs, and large chunks of Proverbs.

Division

On Solomon's death, a civil war breaks out. The "Promised Land" splits into two countries. The ten northern tribes form the kingdom of Israel, the two southern tribes the kingdom of Judah. During the next 300 years, the two nations are constantly attacked by powerful enemies. Israel and Judah have a succession of good and bad kings (mainly bad). In Israel, the kings come from many different families and succeed each other in many different ways (often through murder and assassination). In Judah, God keeps his promise to David, and all the kings are drawn from his family line.

In an attempt to turn his people around, God sends **the prophets**, people such as Elijah and Elisha. The prophets warn of dire consequences if people don't obey God. Some look far into the future and start talking of an anointed leader – a special, chosen one from the descendants of King David who will rescue his people. This is the origin of the idea of **the messiah**.

This story is told in 1 and 2 Kings, and in 2 Chronicles.

Exile and return

The warnings of the prophets largely go unheeded. In 722 BC the northern kingdom of Israel is captured. The Assyrians destroy the country and take the people away.

The southern kingdom limps on for 150 years or so. But it too is attacked by an empire – this time the Babylonians. Judah is overwhelmed and its people are taken into captivity in Babylon, the period known as **the exile**.

In exile, the Jews have to come to terms with the magnitude of their failure. The Temple lies in ruins, Jerusalem is in ashes, and the dream of the Promised Land seems to have ended. But God has not forgotten his promise. Through prophets such as Ezekiel and Jeremiah he promises restoration.

Their exile lasts seventy years. Then, Cyrus the Persian defeats the Babylonians and allows a group of Jews to return to their country and rebuild Jerusalem. Over the next century or so, various groups of exiles return to their homeland. Rebuilding their country is hard, but eventually the city is restored and a new Temple is built.

But the glory days have gone. God sends no more prophets and Israel remains at the mercy of invading nations, first the Greeks and then the mighty Roman empire. Increasingly, the people of Israel place their hopes in the long-awaited messiah.

This story is covered in much of the Old Testament. 2 Kings and 2 Chronicles cover the downfall, Ezra and Nehemiah the return. The so-called "major prophets" – Ezekiel, Jeremiah, and Isaiah – all cover this period, as do many of the "minor prophets", such as Daniel, Haggai, and Zechariah. After this we're at the end of the Old Testament story.

Between the testaments

Between the final book of the Old Testament and the first book of the New lies a period of around 400 years. During this time Judea, as it is known, becomes a minor state under a succession of empires. Some of these attempted to wipe out the Jewish faith, leading to uprisings among the Jews and a brief period of independence. Eventually this independence is brought to an end by the Romans, who conquer the region and put in place a client king called Herod the Great. He builds a magnificent new temple in Jerusalem.

Some of the story of Judea during this period is covered in the Apocrypha, particularly the brief period of independence that is narrated in 1 and 2 Maccabees.

Jesus of Nazareth

A young woman called Mary is told by an angel that she will have a baby. When she tells him, her fiancé, Joseph, prepares to divorce her. But he is told in a dream that her story is true. The baby – named Jesus – is born in Bethlehem. The family have to flee to Egypt to escape the wrath of King Herod (who fears that a new prince has been born). Later, Jesus' family return to Nazareth, where he is brought up. He follows his father's trade as a carpenter and builder.

Jesus' public work begins when he is around thirty years old. His relative, John, starts preparing the way, calling people to repent and baptizing them. He is known as **John the Baptist**. Jesus is baptized and then experiences a period of testing in the wilderness. After John is arrested, Jesus goes to Galilee – a region in the north of Judea. He gathers followers, ordinary people known as his **disciples**. Jesus travels around teaching and performing miracles. He forgives people their sins and raises the dead; he challenges the religious establishment.

Eventually he heads south to Jerusalem for a final time. He enters the city in triumph, with the people cheering and waving palm leaves. This event is

commemorated on **Palm Sunday**. But the authorities
want him dead. He is betrayed by one of his
followers, tried by the Jewish and Roman authorities,
taken outside the city, and executed. This is **the
crucifixion**.

Three days later, his followers start to make
remarkable claims. They say he has risen from
the dead, and appeared to many of them, and this
continues for forty days. They are witnessing **the
resurrection**.

*This story is narrated in the four Gospels: Matthew, Mark,
Luke, and John.*

The first followers

Jesus takes his followers to the Mount of Olives, where
he goes up into heaven. He has told them to wait
for a new helper, the Holy Spirit, who will empower
them. Some fifty days later, during the Jewish festival
of **Pentecost**, the Holy Spirit descends on Jesus'
followers, who start spreading the gospel, the good
news about Jesus.

At first they attend the Temple and the synagogues,
but soon the authorities start to clamp down on them.
When persecution breaks out in Jerusalem some
followers take the gospel north through Samaria
and beyond. Saul, who has led the persecution of
Christians, is miraculously converted. Soon non-Jews
(Gentiles) start to join the church. Peter persuades
Jewish Christians that Gentile Christians shouldn't
have to follow Jewish religious laws.

People like Saul (better known as Paul) and Barnabas start to take the gospel into the very heart of the Roman empire. It spreads to cities including Antioch, where the name "Christians" is first used. The followers meet in houses, led by local men and women. They worship God, pray together, study the Scriptures, and enjoy a shared meal. Part of this meal involves eating bread and drinking wine to remember Jesus' death. This commemoration becomes known as **communion**, the **Lord's Supper**, or the **Eucharist**. They are taught by letters sent from leaders such as Paul and John. These groups of people (much later they will be known as **the church**) look forward to a time when Jesus will return – **the second coming**.

Gradually, however, opposition grows. The Romans grow suspicious of these people. During a visit to Jerusalem, Paul is arrested and, eventually, sent to Rome for trial.

The story of the early church is narrated in the book of Acts. There are also several letters attributed to apostles, including Paul, Peter, and James.

Back to the start

That's almost where the New Testament ends. The final books of the New Testament are written against the backdrop of Roman persecution.

The last book of the New Testament looks far ahead. In exile on a small island, John, one of Jesus' earliest followers, has a vision of the end of time. Jesus will return and gain the final victory over darkness. The world will end as it began – with creation – with God creating a new heaven and a new earth, where all his followers will live in peace.

This is known as **the new heaven and the new earth**. And with this second act of creation, the story contained within the Bible comes to an end.

This is covered by the final book of the Bible: Revelation.

3. Who wrote the Bible?

So that's what the Bible is: a collection of sixty-six books, written at different times and by many different authors, which tells the story of God's relationship with humanity. But how did these books come about? Who wrote them and when? Who decided that something was "Scripture"? And who collected them together in one book and called it "the Bible"? Who "made" the Bible?

The Old Testament: starting with stories

It all begins with stories.

In Genesis, the first book of the Bible, nobody writes a word. Everything in this book – which depicts the origins of the world and the universe – is spoken. God *says* the word, and the world is created; verbal promises are given to Abraham, Isaac, and Jacob.

That's how the Bible was first formed: as *stories* – tales from the deep, deep past, accounts of ancestors and heroes and their encounters with God, the foundational stories of Israel's past. This is known as the oral tradition. It's the base level of the Bible. These stories take different forms: sometimes they are narratives, sometimes poems, and sometimes almost creeds.

Three examples

A tale
One of the most well-known and ancient stories is the tale of Noah and the flood. This story – or versions of it – is widespread among the early civilizations of the East. There's a Phrygian story, a Babylonian account, an Assyrian version... they differ in the details but they agree on one thing: it was very wet. An event like that would linger a long time in the memory. (You can find the biblical account in Genesis 6.)

A poem
The song of Deborah in Judges 5 is an ancient poem that commemorates the defeat of the Canaanite army.

A creed
Deuteronomy 26:5 begins, "My father was a wandering Aramean..." It's a statement about the history of the Israelites, a reminder of where they've come from. Moses instructs them to recite it as part of the worship during their harvest festivals. In religious terminology it's a creed. This must be very early, since in later times the Arameans were sworn enemies of the Jews, and no Jew would want to claim any kind of kinship with them. (The full text is in Deuteronomy 26:1–11.)

There are a number of reasons why the Bible originates with stories, the most obvious one being that hardly anyone could read or write. People learnt by listening and remembering. In cultures such as these, important tales have to be properly learnt and carefully handed on from generation to generation.

Another reason is that the concept of "story" is fundamental to the Bible and, indeed, to the whole of human life. That, above all, is what the Bible is: it is one big story woven of many different strands.

Writing it down

Sooner or later, though, spoken stories have to be written down. And in Exodus (the second book of the Bible) we see this in action: "When Moses went and told the people all the Lord's words and laws, they responded with one voice, 'Everything the Lord has said we will do.' Moses then wrote down everything the Lord had said" (Exodus 24:3–4).

Moses records God's words "on a scroll as something to be remembered" (Exodus 17:14). More famously, on Mount Sinai, the Law is engraved on two "tablets of stone inscribed by the finger of God" (Exodus 31:18).

We don't know exactly when this happened. Some parts were written down earlier than others. According to the Bible itself, the first part to be recorded was the Law of God – inscribed on stone tablets by God himself. And early on in the Israelites' occupation of Canaan, Joshua builds an altar and reads, "all that is written in the book of the Law" to the people (Joshua 23:6).

A brief history of writing

Carved stone and cuneiform tablets

Writing began around 3000 BC, when the Egyptians and Sumerians carved symbols or pictures on stone. Later, an easier, more portable method was developed, which involved making indentations into clay tablets, which were then baked – cuneiform script. These tablets were used to record laws, historical documents, stories, and religious writings. Huge collections of these tablets have been discovered by archaeologists, shedding a lot of light on the world of the Old Testament.

Papyrus and scrolls

Around the seventh century BC, the scroll took over. Scrolls were long rolls of papyrus or parchment. Papyrus was made from papyrus reeds, which could be turned into a thin, light material, ideal for writing. Parchment was made from the skin of animals, such as deer or sheep, scraped and scraped until it formed a thin material. These were made into long strips, 8 to

10 inches high and up to 35 feet long. Generally, scribes would write in two columns and use only one side. The Old Testament books were all scrolls, which is why the books of Kings, Samuel, and Chronicles were split into two – they were too big to fit on one scroll.

Books

Around the first century AD a new medium for writing was invented: the book, or codex. Codices were originally two pieces of thin wood joined together with leather strips. People would write on each side of the wood. Later someone realized that you could get the same effect by taking a sheet of papyrus and simply folding it in half. And then, if you took a number of these sheets and sewed them together, you could make a book.

All of this means that the ancient world thought about writing and publication in a very different way than we do. Everything was handwritten, first on scrolls, and later, codices. The Bible did not become a book – in the sense of a completed collection of lots of pages between two covers – until around AD 300.

How old is the Old Testament?

But when did this happen? Dating these very early
parts is difficult because many books of the Old
Testament are not "one" document but composite
books, edited together by different hands.

Sometimes this is obvious – as, for example, in the
case of Psalms or Proverbs, which contain collections
by different authors. But it also happened elsewhere,
most notably in the Torah. For example, right at the
beginning of the Bible, in Genesis, there are two
accounts of creation. In the first, you get the six days
of creation culminating in the creation of man and
woman and God resting on the seventh day. But then
there is another account. In this version, the days have
disappeared. We get a very brief account of the wider
creation, and then God forms Adam, the first man, from
the dust of the ground while, apparently, the earth is
without any form of vegetation. God then gives Adam
a garden and the animals for his companions, and
then, when this is not enough, he forms Eve from one
of Adam's ribs.

There are obvious differences. Things happen in
a different order. In one account Eve is formed at the
same time; in the other she arrives later.

And there's another significant difference. In the
first account God is referred to by the Hebrew word
"Elohim"; in the second account the word is "YHWH"
(which is probably to be read "Yahweh" – in the
original Hebrew the vowels were never written).

Most English Bibles try to reflect this difference: you will find these two words rendered respectively as "God" and "the Lord".

In fact, in the first five books of the Bible there are several points where variant accounts are given. Sometimes the details between two versions of the story differ slightly. Sometimes the terminology is different; for example, Mount Sinai is also called Mount Horeb.

The implication is that these books have been compiled from various accounts that use different terminology or come from different traditions. Some scholars disagree with this theory. They argue that the Bible exists in the way it has always existed – whole and entire. They are also more likely to sign up to the traditional view of one author: that these books were written by Moses.

But the most widely accepted theory is that several different ancient sources were woven together to form the Torah. They were compiled by an editor (the technical term is "redactor"), probably during the exile in Babylon.

There are various theories about how this was achieved. But regardless of who wrote it down, it is useful to remember the following:

- **Compilation is not the same as invention**
  The texts that were being woven together had been in existence for a long time. They were not necessarily written during the exile.

- **The editors worked hard to be inclusive**
  Clearly those compiling the Torah wanted to
  honour these different traditions. It would have
  been easy for them to choose one account over
  another, but they strove to include as much as
  possible, even when it didn't fit neatly.

We can see this process in place in other parts of the
Old Testament as well.

Some of the History books, for example, draw on
a variety of sources – as, indeed, all historians have
before and since. There are mentions of other sources,
reference works, which were obviously used in writing
the Histories but which are now lost.

Lost books of the Bible

The Bible lists several lost books:

- The book of the Wars of the Lord (Numbers
  21:14)
- The book of Jashar (Joshua 10:13; 2 Samuel 1:18)
- The book of the Annals of Solomon (1 Kings
  11:41)
- The book of the Annals of the Kings of Israel
  (e.g. 1 Kings 14:19; 15:31; 16:5; 16:14)
- The book of the Annals of the Kings of Judah
  (e.g. 1 Kings 14:29; 15:7; 15:23)
- The book of the Annals (Nehemiah 12:23).

Other books appear to combine different sources. The book of Daniel, for example, is written in two different languages: Hebrew and Aramaic. Again, some scholars would argue for its essential unity, but others say it has been stitched together from two different sources.

Some books combine collections from different authors. The book of Proverbs includes collections attributed to Solomon, Agur the son of Jakeh, King Lemuel's mother, and some to a being known only as "the Oracle". The "men of Hezekiah" are also credited with compiling some of the book. There are also sections simply attributed to "the wise".

Other books have been compiled from the same source or author. The book of Haggai, for example, is a collection of oracles by one author – the prophet Haggai – but given at different dates. (This kind of compilation is common among the prophetic books.)

Of course, not all the books of the Old Testament are composite, edited documents. But certainly the majority of them have had some element of editorial control. At some point, they were edited together: redacted. They didn't spring from the pen of one writer in one high-powered session.

The New Testament: starting with stories

Like the Old Testament, the New Testament begins with stories remembered about Jesus: things he did, stuff he said. This information comes from people who encountered Jesus. These eyewitnesses travelled from church to church, talking about what they had seen and heard.

Some of these stories were learnt by heart, passed on from one Christian to another. There is even an account of this in action. It comes from a letter which Paul wrote to the Christians at Corinth:

> *For I received from the Lord what I also passed on to you: The Lord Jesus, on the night he was betrayed, took bread, and when he had given thanks, he broke it and said, "This is my body, which is for you; do this in remembrance of me." In the same way, after supper he took the cup, saying, "This cup is the new covenant in my blood; do this, whenever you drink it, in remembrance of me." For whenever you eat this bread and drink this cup, you proclaim the Lord's death until he comes.*
>
> **1 Corinthians 11:23–26**

Paul was told an important story; he committed it to memory and now he's passing it on to others.

The stories and even the teaching of the apostles were considered to have some kind of authority and power. For example, Paul, writing to the Thessalonians, says this: "when you received the word of God, which you heard from us, you accepted it not as a human word, but as it actually is, the word of God, which is indeed at work in you who believe" (1 Thessalonians 2:13–14).

What Paul proclaimed to them was, presumably, the

good news about Jesus, and perhaps some evidence and teaching from Old Testament texts.

So the New Testament also begins with a base layer of oral tradition. At some stage stories and sayings of Jesus were written down. It probably happened quite early – it seems very unlikely that the first Christians waited decades before committing anything about Jesus to paper. So, by the time the Gospels came to be written – probably in the AD 60s – a number of written resources may have been available. We don't know exactly what these were, but scholars have suggested:

- a collection of the sayings of Jesus in Aramaic, made by the church in Judea

- a collection of miracle stories

- an earlier "Gospel" in Aramaic

- a passion narrative – that is, an account of the last week of Jesus' life

- a document of Jesus' teachings, which scholars today call Q (see below)

- collections of parables, such as the group that fills Mark 4 or the parables of Luke 15 which all centre on the theme of something being "lost".

And from these sources, the Gospels were written.

The earliest evidence
The earliest actual manuscript copy of any New
Testament work is a fragment of John 18, written
on papyrus. It has been dated to AD 100.

The synoptic gospels

In the opening to his Gospel, Luke describes his
research method:

*Many have undertaken to draw up an account of the
things that have been fulfilled among us, just as they
were handed down to us by those who from the first
were eyewitnesses and servants of the word. With this
in mind, since I myself have carefully investigated
everything from the beginning, I too decided to
write an orderly account for you, most excellent
Theophilus, so that you may know the certainty of the
things you have been taught.*
Luke 1:1–4

Several things are obvious:

- He's writing an orderly account, arranging his
  material.

- He's following in the footsteps of others. "Many"
  apparently have had a crack at writing something
  about Jesus.

- The material is drawn from eyewitnesses.

- He has made his own investigations.

- He is writing to convince someone of the truth about Jesus – in this case a high-ranking Roman official called Theophilus.

For Luke, at least, but most likely for all the Gospels, this gives us clues about their composition. The Gospels weren't thrown together or created in a sudden burst of divine enlightenment. They were well-researched works, carefully structured and arranged.

The Gospel writers made choices about what information to include and how to arrange it. Sometimes they differ: Matthew, for example, puts together a lot of material in one setting – it forms chapters 5–7 of his Gospel in our Bibles and we call it the Sermon on the Mount. Where Luke uses the same material, he spreads it out more widely throughout his Gospel.

Broadly speaking, there is a great deal of agreement between the first three Gospels – Matthew, Mark, and Luke. These are termed the "synoptic gospels". The term comes from the Latin *syn* ("one") and *optic* ("seeing"). They see events from one perspective and follow the same overall chronological arrangement.

How do we explain this close relationship? The most popular theory is that Luke and Matthew used Mark as the basis for their Gospels. As with any theory about biblical authorship, there are a bewildering number of different opinions, but it's generally accepted that Mark was written first. It's the shortest Gospel, for one thing, and shows the least sign of editing. (For example, there is a tendency in Matthew and Luke to explain things a bit more.)

So Mark is written first, and then Matthew and Luke use that Gospel as one of their core sources. But they have other sources as well. There are many passages and sayings that appear in Matthew and Luke but not in Mark. These, scholars suggest, come from another document, a collection of Jesus' sayings, which they call "Q".

"Q"

The initial comes from the German word *Quelle*, meaning "source". Scholars make great claims for Q. They end up talking about the Q community and even attempt to make subdivisions within Q itself. But we should bear in mind that it is a hypothetical document. No one has ever seen a copy of Q; no fragments of it have ever been found.

Along with Mark and "Q", both Luke and Matthew have their own unique sources, with stories and sayings of Jesus that only appear in their Gospels.

John's Gospel

The Gospel of John is very different. It's generally assumed to have been written later. It does draw on some of the same sources as the other Gospels, but also has its own fount of sayings and stories. The author of John refers to these: he writes that "Jesus did many other signs in the presence of his disciples, which are not recorded in this book" (John 20:30). He says, "Jesus did many other things as well. If every one of them were written down, I suppose that even the whole world would not have room for the books that would be written" (John 21:25).

So not everything that Jesus said and did ended up in the Gospels. We know that other stories and sayings circulated. Some of these turn up elsewhere. For example, in Acts 20, Paul quotes a saying of Jesus: "It is more blessed to give than to receive" (Acts 20:35). But this saying doesn't appear in any of the Gospels.

The Gospels, like the Torah, are therefore composite documents, drawn together from various collections and sources. But the base of all these accounts is the eyewitness testimony of the things that Jesus said and did.

The letters

The stories and sayings of Jesus – in various collections – were not the only things circulating among the early church. There were other things as well:

- Romans 1:3–4 contains what is probably a portion of an early Jewish Christian statement of faith.
- Philippians 2:5–11, which is a hymn or poem, tells the story of who Jesus was and what he did.

Most of all, the early church leaders sent each other letters.

There are twenty-two letters in the New Testament, including Revelation, which, although not using the traditional letter format, was clearly sent round to various churches.

Some of the letters date from earlier than the completed Gospels. The earliest of Paul's letters is probably Galatians, assuming it was written after his visit to the region in AD 48/49 and before the Jerusalem council of AD 49. The rest of his letters were written between AD 50 and his death in the mid AD 60s. Of the non-Pauline letters, James's is probably the earliest.

The letters would have been written on papyrus or sometimes parchment. This would have been rolled and put in a container, and then hand-delivered by a trusted messenger such as a servant, friend, or business associate. Letters were normally dictated to a scribe, but the author might add a greeting in his own hand. Normally, a copy would be made which was kept by the writer.

Once the letter had been read by its intended recipient, it might be copied and passed on, especially if the writer were an important man like Paul. In fact, in his letter to the church at Colossae, he writes, "After the letter has been read to you, see that it is also read in the church of the Laodiceans and that you in turn read the letter from Laodicea" (Colossians 4:16). These materials, then – the Gospel accounts, Luke's history of the early church (Acts), and various letters from early church leaders – were eventually to come together to form the Christian Scriptures or New Testament.

4. Who put the Bible together?

When a shepherd called Amos delivered a prophecy sometime between 780 and 740 BC, he never imagined he was doing something that would end up bound between the covers of a big black book, or even carefully written on a scroll. According to the book itself, he was just obeying orders: the Lord told him to "Go, prophesy to my people Israel" (Amos 7:15).

Similarly, some 800 years later, when the apostle Paul wrote a letter to the misbehaving church at Corinth, he didn't know he was writing the "New Testament". He was just writing "not to shame you but to warn you" (1 Corinthians 4:14).

Yet what they spoke and wrote ended up as Scripture. So how did that happen? Who decided what made it into the Bible? How did documents as varied as the poetry of Psalms, the letters of Paul, or the prophecies of Isaiah come to make up "the Bible"?

From texts to Tanakh
The first part of the Bible to be accepted as Scripture was the Law, the Torah. When the Jews returned to Jerusalem from their exile in Babylon, Ezra gathered the people together and read out "the Book of the Law

of Moses" (Nehemiah 8:1). So by the sixth century BC, the Torah is in place.

But other writings were also collected together during the exile – histories, prophecies, and poetry. Around the same time the Torah was put together, a collection that has been termed the "former" or "early" prophets was made. The name is confusing, since it included books of history such as Joshua, Judges, Samuel, and Kings. After the exile, this section – the Prophets, or the Nevi'im – grew to accommodate Isaiah, Jeremiah, and Ezekiel, and a section known as "The Twelve", which is also known as the "Minor Prophets".

The final section of the Tanakh to be decided was the Ketuvim, or Writings, and this brought together books of wisdom, history, and stuff that just didn't seem to fit anywhere else. This was the final set of books to be admitted, although books like the Psalms had been used for a long time.

By the fourth century BC, the Torah and the Nevi'im had probably been standardized, and most of the Ketuvim was also in place. But there was still debate about some books, and each Jewish group had a different view of their status. Every Jewish group accepted the Torah as Scripture, but beyond that there was a degree of fluidity. The Sadducees – the people running the Temple in Jesus' day – did not accept the scriptural authority of anything other than the Torah, while the Pharisees accepted books such as Psalms and the Prophets. And the famous Dead Sea Scrolls – the treasured library of a Jewish community at Qumran

– contain fragments from every book of the Hebrew scriptures except one: Esther. Clearly Esther was not a part of their "Bible".

Jesus, certainly, used more than just the Torah. Jesus quotes from some twenty-four books of the Hebrew scriptures, and he says that he did not come to abolish "the Law or the Prophets" (Matthew 5:17).

In fact, it was not until the late first century AD that the Old Testament took its final definitive form.

In AD 66 the Jews rebelled against Rome. The outcome was catastrophic: the Romans besieged and recaptured Jerusalem and destroyed the Temple. According to Jewish tradition, before the final conflict, a group of rabbis left Jerusalem and settled in Jamnia or Jabneh, some 12 miles south of Jaffa. There they addressed the thorny question of what writings made up the official canon of Hebrew scriptures.

By then most of the books were accepted. But there were arguments over some of the more problematic books such as Song of Songs (a love poem) and Esther (which doesn't mention God).

In the end there were three main criteria which made for a book's inclusion.

- **Tradition.** Books such as the Psalms and the Major Prophets had been used in synagogues for many years. They were obviously Scripture.

- **Association with a well-known figure.** Song of

Songs might be a bit racy, but it was associated with Solomon.

- **Association with a Jewish festival.** Esther's story was celebrated in the festival of Purim.

The debate took a long time and was not properly decided until around AD 90. The list that emerged was the list of scriptures we find in our Old Testament today.

Canon

The word "canon" means the official, standard list. It comes originally from the Hebrew, meaning "reed". (We also use it for the word "cane".) These straight reeds were used as measuring rods, so the word canon can be used to imply a rule of faith. When we talk of the canon of Scripture, we mean those books that conform to a certain set of rules.

From books to Bible

The creation of the Christian canon also took a long time and in many ways underwent a similar process to that of the Old Testament's creation.

But before the New Testament was written, the first followers of Jesus used the Hebrew scriptures – the Old Testament – but in a Greek translation known as the Septuagint.

The Septuagint

"Septuagint" comes from the Latin phrase *Interpretatio septuaginta virorum* – "translation of the seventy interpreters". The name comes from the legend that, when seventy-two translators gathered together in Alexandria, Egypt, to translate the Hebrew scriptures into Greek, they each, individually, came up with an identical translation.

More likely the translation took place over many decades, beginning with the Torah, with the rest of the Hebrew scriptures added later. There were large Jewish communities outside Judea who couldn't speak Hebrew. If the Jewish faith was going to mean anything to these people, then they needed the Law – the Torah – to be translated into Greek, the common language of the Mediterranean world. Since Greek was so widely spoken, this translation become the most widely read version of the Hebrew scriptures of its day.

There are differences between the Septuagint and the Hebrew text. The Septuagint uses a different version of the Tanakh than the Hebrew version, which later became the authoritative text. It also has more books in it. There are thirteen books in the Septuagint that are not in the Hebrew canon, as well as additional chapters to Esther and Daniel, and an extra psalm. These books are what later became known as the Apocrypha.

Soon, though, as we've seen, they began to add their own sacred writings in the form of the Gospels and letters.

From very early on, the four Gospels were considered the most important items. Around AD 150, Justin Martyr wrote about the primacy of the "memoirs of the apostles", while a little later, Irenaeus of Lyons (writing around AD 170–180) argued that, of the different accounts of Jesus' life, only Matthew, Mark, Luke, and John were "true and reliable". These Gospels were joined in the approved lists by the works of other apostles – the letters of Paul and other well-known Christian figures.

And so the Christian scriptures began to take shape. Gradually, a consensus emerged. There was still some discussion about certain books, particularly Jude, 2 Peter, 2 and 3 John, and Revelation. In the spring of AD 367, Bishop Athanasius of Alexandria distributed a letter that listed what he considered the canonical books of the Christian Bible. And this is the first time that the twenty-seven books we find in modern Bibles were listed as a definitive canon. Although there were still the odd variants, the basic shape of the New Testament was pretty much fixed from then on: the Gospels, Acts, twenty-one letters, and the mysterious book of Revelation.

Marcion

Athanasius' list was not the first by any means. The earliest surviving suggestion of what books should constitute Christian "scriptures" comes from a heretic – a man called Marcion – in AD 144. Marcion was vehemently anti-Semitic, so he omitted anything Jewish. That meant jettisoning the entire Old Testament and every Gospel except for Luke's (and even then he edited bits out he didn't like). He did include some letters of Paul (Paul was Greek, so that made him OK). But even though the wider church condemned Marcion, they refused to be rushed into providing an alternative list. They knew he was wrong, but they still hadn't come to the final conclusion on what was right. There is a list called the Muratorian Canon, which includes the books that we know as the traditional New Testament, but scholars disagree on whether this list comes from AD 170 or much later.

Thus the Bible that we have today "grew". No single person decided on the contents. It took centuries of debate and discussion among Jewish and Christian theologians to decide on what was Scripture.

The first Bibles

In the fourth century AD, the first, proper, bound Bibles were produced, probably in Alexandria. These volumes – the Codex Sinaiticus, Codex Alexandrinus and Codex Vaticanus – are wonderful pieces of technology. You can see the Codex Sinaiticus and the Codex Alexandrinus in the British Library. They contain the Septuagint and the New Testament books, but they also contain some books that did not make it into the final selection: Sinaiticus contains the epistle of Barnabas and the Shepherd of Hermas; Alexandrinus contains 1 and 2 Clement. Nevertheless these are the first instances of the Bible as a "book".

The inspired word of God?

All of which raises an important issue: if so many human agencies were involved in the creation, editing, and compilation of the Bible, then is it still sacred? Is it still to be considered the inspired word of God?

First, we have to understand that, although Christians talk about the authority of the Bible, these books are not authoritative because they are in the Bible. They were collected together because they were considered authoritative. This is an important distinction. We must remember that *the authority of the individual text came first.*

These books were considered special, before anyone thought of collecting them together in one volume. They all made it into the Bible because believers felt that, in some fashion, these words written by humans were, in fact, the words of God. They were inspired.

In Paul's second letter to Timothy, he writes that Scripture is *theopneustos* – "God-breathed": "All Scripture is God-breathed and is useful for teaching, rebuking, correcting and training in righteousness, so that the servant of God may be thoroughly equipped for every good work" (2 Timothy 3:16–17).

This is where the idea of inspiration comes from. "Inspire" comes from the Latin *inspirare*, meaning "to breathe, or blow into". When Christians talk about the Bible being inspired, then, they are stating that it comes from God; it contains, as it were, the breath of God. And this is an idea that the Bible also claims for itself. The words of the prophets, for example, are often introduced with a kind of formula: "the word of the Lord that came to so-and-so". The phrase "the Lord spoke" or "Thus says the Lord" occurs more than 3,800 times in the Old Testament alone. And we have already seen Paul make similar claims for the message that he spoke to the people in Thessalonica.

The fundamental Christian belief is that the Scriptures are a message from God: that, in the words of the First Vatican Council, "they have God as their author".

But that, in turn, begs another question: how did that happen? How did God "breathe" this book? How did the author get to work?

Over the years, Christians and Jews have proposed many theories about the mechanics of divine inspiration. Although the idea of the complete truthfulness of Scripture has been part of their belief from the beginning, there is not one uniform understanding among believers as to how the Bible is inspired.

Some Christians believe in a kind of divine dictation: that God simply dictated what he wanted to be written down. Therefore, all the author did was write down as he was told from God, and the end product is the word of God. It must, therefore, be both infallible and inerrant, that is, it cannot be in error, and it contains no faults. This is the stance that is adopted by the more fundamentalist churches.

At the other end of the spectrum is the idea that the books were composed by purely human means, but later were recognized as being inspired and given a kind of stamp of approval by God (and the church).

Most Christians take a more middle-ground view, believing that while God inspired and guided the writers through the Holy Spirit, he allowed them the freedom to use their own language, experience, and knowledge. Again we can see this at work in the Bible. The personalities of authors are clearly reflected in the way that they communicate their message. They write in their own style. Jeremiah and Ezekiel were writing at roughly the same time, but no one could mistake the style of one for the other. And the biblical writers research and report stories from other sources. In the Old Testament, Ezra quotes from the Persian archives (Ezra 7:11–26), while in the New Testament, Luke's account of the composition of his Gospel clearly shows that he selected and arranged his material.

In that sense it lines up with another core Christian idea: the incarnation of Jesus. Christians hold that Jesus was, at the same time, both fully God and fully human. In the same way the Bible is both divinely inspired and written by humans.

Those who wrote and edited the Bible were not automatons. Luke was a painstaking historian. Whoever put together the Talmud took care over the selection and arrangement of their material. They also – as we have seen – wrote in their own distinctive styles. God honours the artistry, craftsmanship, and intelligence of humanity. This human involvement also reminds us that the Bible is not only a record of what God is like; it is also a record of what human beings are like – even those human beings who penned its words.

But let's go back to that quote from Paul's letter to Timothy. The result of Scripture being "God-breathed", he says, is that it equips people to take action. This is a book that changes people. What makes the Bible unique, for Christians, is that it is active, alive. The writer of Hebrews says, "the word of

God is alive and active... it judges the thoughts and attitudes of the heart" (Hebrews 4:12).

There is a tale told in East Africa about a village woman who always used to walk around with her Bible. "Why are you always reading that?" her neighbours teased her. "There are so many other books you could read." The woman replied, "I know there are many books I could read. But this is the only book which reads me."

For Christians, the Bible is more than a text; it is a truly interactive book. It challenges, inspires, thrills, excites, and changes all those who read it.

For them, the Bible is more than just another book: it is the word of God.

5. The Bible: book by book

To recap, the Bible is arranged in two parts – the Old and New Testaments – and then further subdivided into different sections.

The Old Testament consists of Law (Torah), Histories, Wisdom, Major Prophets, and Minor Prophets. The New Testament includes Gospels and Acts, letters of Paul, other letters, and Revelation.

These books are written in a wide variety of different styles and attributed to many different authors. But what could you expect to find in each book?

To help you get an idea, here is a *very* brief guide to each book.

The Old Testament: the Law

The first five books of the Bible are known as the Law, the Torah, or the Books of Moses. Torah – the Jewish name for this section – means "law", "teachings", or "instruction", and these five books form the material on which Judaism was (and is) based. The books introduce some of the core themes of the Bible, such as creation, sin, and the relationship between humanity and God.

Genesis

Genesis is the book of beginnings. Everything starts here. Genesis contains some of the most famous Bible stories: as well as the creation stories, there are tales including Noah's flood, Jacob's ladder, and Joseph and his famous coat. It also tells the origins of the Jewish people (and everyone else for that matter) and the stories of their patriarchs – people such as Abraham, Isaac, Jacob, and Joseph. These stories tell us about the relationship between God and humanity, underlined by the covenant, or promise, of God to be with his people and to give them the land.

Exodus

The title of the book means "exit". (It's from the Greek title *Exodos Aigyptou* which means "departure from Egypt".) It introduces Moses and shows him leading the Israelites from slavery to freedom. We see the burning bush, the ten plagues, the origin of Passover, the parting of the Red Sea, and the giving of the Ten Commandments. The big theme of Exodus is God's rescue of the people from slavery in Egypt. Because God has rescued them, they are to follow him and obey his laws – many of which are included in the book.

Leviticus

Leviticus is named after the tribe of the Levites, which supplied all the priests for Israel (although, actually, the Levites appear in only two verses in the book: Leviticus

25:32–33). This is essentially their priestly handbook. Some ancient rabbis called the book *torat kohanim*, the manual of the priests, which more or less sums it up. Leviticus is not an easy read, but it is important, because it contains many rules and principles by which Jews live today, such as the importance of sabbath, and the festivals still celebrated by millions of Jews.

Numbers

This book gets its name from the census lists of people in each tribe – but they occupy only a small part of the book (two chapters: 1 and 26). It continues the story of the exodus. It's a travel book, telling the story of a journey that takes the Israelites from Sinai to the borders of Canaan. There, instead of entering the land, they lose heart and decide not to bother. This results in them wandering in the wilderness for forty years. It has a lot about the tabernacle, which was a kind of portable, flat-pack temple.

Deuteronomy

This is Moses' farewell speech. He reminds the people of all that God has done for them and the laws that he has given them to live by. Indeed, the name "Deuteronomy" means "repetition of the law". More than any other book of the Bible, Deuteronomy forms the basis of Judaism – both at the time of Jesus and ever since. It contains Judaism's most famous prayer – the *Shema* (Deuteronomy 6:4–9) – and what is probably their most ancient creed (Deuteronomy

26:5–10). Jesus quotes more from Deuteronomy than from any other Hebrew scripture.

The Old Testament: the Histories

The next section of the Bible covers the history of Israel, from the conquest of Canaan through to their exile in Babylon and their return. Other books of the Bible also contain historical accounts (Jeremiah, for example), so this is not the only place that you'll find history in the Bible. But these books focus on the historical narrative.

Joshua

The book takes its name from its hero, Joshua, successor to Moses. It tells how the Israelites finally cross the Jordan and conquer Canaan, the land that God has given them. There are many battles, including the famous collapse of the walls of Jericho and the destruction of Ai and Hazor. The book concludes with the death of Joshua, and also with the Israelites never quite completing the job.

Judges

After Joshua's death there was a time of anarchy, typified by the repeated phrase, "In those days Israel had no king; everyone did as they saw fit" (Judges 21:25). In some ways, it is a strikingly modern book. Even some of the judges themselves – people such as Samson and Gideon – are deeply flawed.

Ruth

Set in the time of the judges, during a period of
peace between Israel and Moab, this is a kind of love
story, a tale about family duty, affection, and a loyalty
and commitment that go beyond the boundaries of
duty or legal obligation. Despite being a Moabite,
Ruth accompanies her mother-in-law Naomi back to
Canaan. "Where you go, I will go, and where you stay, I
will stay. Your people will be my people and your God
my God," she says (Ruth 1:16).

1 and 2 Samuel

1 and 2 Samuel is actually one book split into two
because it would not fit on one scroll. The first half
tells the story of the rise to power of the first two
kings of Israel, Saul and his rival, David. We also meet
Samuel, the first prophet. The second part tells the
story of the rise and fall of King David, of the conflict
within his household and his personal failure and
sin. It is the story of how Israel's greatest king gains
control of the kingdom, only to lose control of himself
and his family. He commits adultery with Bathsheba
and then has her husband, Uriah, killed during battle.
Faced with personal failure and sin, he throws himself
on God's mercy.

1 and 2 Kings

These books (again, one work split into two) take the
history on from David, through the reign of Solomon

and on to the splitting of the kingdom into two
separate nations: Israel in the north and Judah in the
south. The two kingdoms have many kings and rulers,
each judged good or bad according to whether
they obeyed God. (Mostly, they don't.) Kings also
describes the rise of the prophets, God's spokesmen
who hold those in power to account. It ends with
the destruction of both kingdoms: Israel in 722 BC,
destroyed by the Assyrians; Judah in 586 BC, crushed
by the Babylonians. The Temple is destroyed and the
majority of the population taken away to Babylon.

1 and 2 Chronicles

Chronicles repeats the history of Israel and Judah as
given in Samuel and Kings. But Chronicles is much
less critical of David and Solomon (for instance, there
is no mention of the seven-year civil war, and nothing
at all about Bathsheba). And it's not really interested
in the northern kingdom of Israel, but with Judah.
Written after the exile in Babylon, Chronicles is a
kind of highlights package, aiming to show that the
Judah that was re-established after the exile was a
continuation of the past. It also focuses on those kings
who choose to live godly lives, giving extensive
treatment to good, reforming kings such as Hezekiah,
Jehoshaphat, Joash, and Asa. But perhaps the main
"character" in the book is not a human at all, but the
Temple itself. This is a book in which the worship of
God is central.

Ezra and Nehemiah

These two books tell of the series of returns, of various groups of exiled Jews, from Babylon to Judah. In Ezra, Jews led by Zerubbabel return to Jerusalem and start rebuilding the Temple. Then Ezra returns with another lot and calls the people back to God. The book of Nehemiah continues the narrative, with the story of the third return to Jerusalem, when a group of exiles under Nehemiah make their way back to their homeland. The work there has ground to a halt (again) and the walls have not been repaired. Under his influence and inspiration, the walls are repaired in just fifty-two days. These books are not just about rebuilding Jerusalem; they are also about restoring the faith, re-establishing the ancient festivals, and rededicating the nation to God.

Esther

Esther is a romantic adventure story. An evil man called Mordecai schemes to murder all the Jews in Susa, in Persia. But Esther, a Jew, becomes queen and foils the plot. Esther is a book about liberation and rescue. It shows how God works behind the scenes to rescue his people. This rescue is still celebrated today in the festival of Purim, described in the final chapter of the book.

The Old Testament: Wisdom books

The next five books of the Bible are very different to
the histories and contain poetry, collections of sayings,
and philosophical writings.

Job

Job is a profound, powerful meditation on a basic
human dilemma: why do good people suffer? The book
is set in the time of the patriarchs, but Job himself lives
in "the land of Uz", which is somewhere in "the East"
(Job 1:1, 3). So he's not an Israelite – appropriate for
such a universal question. The book takes the form of
a dialogue between Job and various not-so-helpful
friends. Significantly, it rejects easy answers. Instead of
nice, neat solutions to why suffering occurs, in the end,
God sweeps in, washing away all the arguments and
the shallow theories with the reality of his power and
presence.

Psalms

Psalms is a poetry anthology, or songbook. Brought
together over at least 400 years, and written by
different authors, the book served as a prayer book
for use in the Temple and synagogues. The 150
psalms cover subjects including war, peace, betrayal,
loneliness, suffering, joy, and worship – all human
life is here. Psalms is one of the most emotional and
personal books of the Bible. Reading it is often like
peeking into someone's spiritual journal: one minute
the air is full of praises; the next, everything is despair.

The raw honesty with which the psalmist faces God is compelling and moving. The Hebrew title is "Praises", and, though not all of the psalms fall into that category, the book as a whole undoubtedly celebrates God, who, in the eyes of the psalmist, is with his people through all of life's joys and hardships.

Proverbs

Proverbs is a book of wise sayings. These are not philosophical musings but practical advice. The Hebrew concept of wisdom was closer to the idea of life skills, providing God's people with advice on how to live a godly life in an ungodly world. These are not arranged thematically: they dart about from one subject to another. Some themes recur: the value of hard work; the importance of controlling your speech; the value of true friendship; the dangers of drink and – ahem – "loose" women; and respect for the poor and needy.

Ecclesiastes

Ecclesiastes is one of the most surprising books of the Bible: a weary summary of the apparent pointlessness of life. The "Teacher" looks at all of life – everything under the sun – and concludes that everything is futile. Having said that, the book also contains some of the most moving, beautiful passages in Scripture. So it's not *all* doom and gloom…

Song of Songs

Another surprise! Song of Songs is a love poem. It is a celebration of the joy of physical love, a song between bridegroom and bride. The metaphors in it are… er… unusual (at one point the woman's hair is likened to a flock of goats) but that's how they did love poetry back then.

The Old Testament: the Prophets

The section of the Bible known as "the Prophets" contains seventeen books. The first five are known as the Major Prophets; the remaining twelve are called the Minor Prophets.

Isaiah

Isaiah is the first of the great books of prophecy in the Bible. The name Isaiah means "the Lord saves", and that sums up the theme of this work. God will judge his people for their sins, but he will also rescue them from captivity. The book is set around the time of the Judean exile, and political observations and historical accounts jostle with visions of the near and far future. Along with warnings to current kings, there are many references to a future ruler, a messiah – the anointed one – who will rescue Israel and usher in a new age of peace and wholeness, when the land will be healed, when there will be no more suffering, sadness, or pain.

Jeremiah

Jeremiah prophesied for nearly fifty years. His key
message was that, unless they changed their ways,
God would punish the inhabitants of the kingdom of
Judah and its capital, Jerusalem. But despite the doom
and gloom of his message, Jeremiah does contain
hope. At one of the lowest points Jeremiah is instructed
to buy a field in territory currently occupied by the
invading Babylonian army: it is a metaphor, a sign that
one day the people will return to their land.

Lamentations

This is a poem. It's the funeral song of a city. In 588 BC
the army of the Babylonian empire overran the city
of Jerusalem and took the people away into exile in
Babylon. Lamentations, traditionally attributed to the
prophet Jeremiah, consists of five poems reflecting the
chaos and despair. The Hebrew name for the book is
simply "Alas", which sums it up perfectly.

Ezekiel

There's a thin line between "prophet" and "nutter",
and sometimes in this thrillingly bizarre book, it
seems as though Ezekiel has crossed that line. He
was among the first group of people from Judah to be
deported to Babylon, and his actions, along with his
vivid visions, are designed to shock God's people out
of their complacency and apathy. So his messages
are hard to ignore. He begins with a weird vision
of creatures in heaven. Each creature has wings,

four faces, and a set of wheels. Sometimes Ezekiel's messages are couched in violent, almost obscene language, or played out in dramatic, bizarre actions. (At one point he lies on his left side for 390 days and on his right side for forty to symbolize the time of the exile. See? You couldn't help but notice him.)

Daniel

Part story, part apocalyptic vision, the first half tells the tale of Daniel and his friends, Jewish captives in Babylon, and of how their refusal to compromise their faith is vindicated and rewarded. It contains such well-known stories as Daniel in the lions' den, the three Jews in the fiery furnace, and the writing on the wall during Belshazzar's feast. The second half is a full-on, Jewish apocalyptic prophecy about future empires, angelic powers, and times of trial. (For this reason some see it as two books welded together.) The book was important in Jesus' time, when Judea was occupied by Roman forces. Images and ideas from Daniel crop up in Jesus' teaching and in Revelation.

Hosea

This was a man who truly lived his message. Hosea was told to marry Gomer, an unfaithful prostitute. She betrays him but he buys her back from slavery. Their relationship was symbolic of God's enduring love. Despite the unfaithfulness of Israel, God will not give up on it. Just as Hosea redeems Gomer, so God will redeem Israel.

Joel

A vast army of locusts has descended on Judah, eating everything in its path and bringing drought and famine. Joel explains that this is a judgment on sin. There will be another judgment – the "day of the Lord" – when God will restore his people, bring abundance and safety to them, and dwell with them.

Amos

Amos was a sheep farmer from Judah, who prophesied against the leaders and people of Israel. He starts with a series of oracles condemning foreign nations, but then he turns to deliver a stinging attack on Israel and their skin-deep religion. They pretend to be holy, but their society is crawling with idolatry, corruption, and injustice. Amos tells them that God hates their empty religion: what he wants is justice and mercy.

Obadiah

This brief prophecy deals with the destruction of Edom, a nation south of the Dead Sea. It should have supported Israel during an invasion (probably the destruction of Jerusalem in 586 BC), but didn't. For that reason it will be punished. With only 291 words in the original Hebrew, Obadiah is the shortest book in the Bible.

Jonah

This is a story *about* a prophet, rather than a book of prophecy. Jonah is given a message: go to Nineveh

– the capital of the Assyrian empire – and tell its people to repent. He goes the other way – to Tarshish – is thrown overboard, and ends up in the belly of a fish. Eventually he goes to Nineveh and delivers his message. We tend to retell it as a children's story, but this is one of the most profound statements about God's love in the entire Scripture. The surprise is not that Jonah ran away; it's that God wants to forgive the Assyrians. How could God care about people who were trying to destroy the Israelites?

Micah

It's a time of relative peace, but Micah says that the day of the Lord is coming and judgment is on its way. In strong, vivid language Micah rails against injustice and calls on the people to change their ways. In one of his most famous passages, Micah looks to a different kind of ruler, a future king who will shepherd his people into a time of great peace.

Nahum

The book describes the destruction of Nineveh, capital of the Assyrian empire. The avenging God is on his way, powerful enough to destroy mountains and dry up seas. God is depicted in Nahum as slow but sure. He is "slow to anger" but his power is enormous.

Habakkuk

Judah was in turmoil; everything was falling apart. So Habakkuk asks God a simple question: why are you allowing this to happen? The question is worked out in two "dialogues" between the prophet and God, before Habakkuk concludes with a prayer-like psalm.

Zephaniah

Zephaniah was a distant relative of King Josiah of Judah, under whom there was something of a national revival. So it's possible that Zephaniah was that rare thing: a prophet to whom people listened. His message is certainly shocking. He says that the day of the Lord is coming. The people of Judah believed that this would be the moment when the Lord would wipe out all their enemies. But Zephaniah tells them that Judah will also get what it deserves.

Haggai

It's 520 BC. The exiled Jews who have returned to Jerusalem have found life hard and the city in ruins. They have abandoned the rebuilding of the Temple. Haggai urges them to review their priorities, lay aside economic concerns, and get the Temple going again. In the struggle for existence, the people have forgotten that God is still to be at the centre of their lives.

Zechariah

This book is part exhortation, part vision. Zechariah urges the people to rebuild the Temple and live in accordance with God's commands – avoiding the fate of their ancestors. The book also weaves together narratives, visions, and oracles to point to the messiah who will be the true anointed ruler of Israel. Few books of the Bible are as difficult to interpret as Zechariah. But no prophet has more to say about the messiah.

Malachi

The Temple has been rebuilt, sacrifices are being offered again, but times are difficult. Old sins are returning. There is corruption, injustice, and greed. The Temple is a place where people simply go through the ritual. Faced with a disheartened, disobedient people, Malachi reminds them that religious ritual has value only if it is a true expression of real belief.

The Apocrypha

Some Bibles, as we've seen, contain the Apocrypha. These are the extra books that were in the Septuagint – the Greek translation of the Tanakh – but not in the Hebrew canon.

1 Maccabees

1 Maccabees tells the story of the Maccabean wars, when the Jewish religion was under threat of destruction by Greek-speaking rulers. The Jews revolted against their rulers, led by Judas Maccabeus (and his family). It also tells the story of the Jewish festival of Hanukkah. It was originally written in Hebrew, probably around 130–100 BC.

2 Maccabees

2 Maccabees is a summary of a lost, five-volume
work by Jason of Cyrene. It details events that led up
to the Maccabean revolt, and the subsequent battles
up to 161 BC. Written sometime between 124 BC and
the arrival of the Romans in 63 BC, it is concerned
with asserting the importance of the Temple and the
Jewish law.

3 Maccabees

Greek Orthodox Bibles also include 3 Maccabees. This
is an account of God's miraculous interventions on
behalf of persecuted Jews in Alexandria, Egypt. It's got
nothing to do with the Maccabees, since the events it
details took place (a) fifty years before the Maccabean
revolt and (b) in Egypt.

Esdras

1 Esdras is a retelling of various portions of Jewish
history, drawing heavily on Chronicles and Ezra.
("Esdras" is the Greek form of the Hebrew name
"Ezra".) 2 Esdras is a piece of apocalyptic writing
trying to explain why God allowed the Romans to
destroy the Jewish Temple in AD 70. It contains writings
from different times and authors, some of which are
later Christian interpolations.

Ecclesiasticus, or The Wisdom of Ben Sirach

This is a wisdom book, a bit like Proverbs. It includes
a famous passage that begins, "Let us now praise

famous men" (Sirach 44:1 – 50:29), which not only mentions great heroes of the Old Testament but also includes the author himself! It was written around 200–180 BC.

The Book of Wisdom, or The Wisdom of Solomon
A Wisdom book that is a kind of positive reply to Ecclesiastes, it talks a lot about the uses of wisdom, particularly in preparing a soul for life after death. Since it was composed in Greek (probably between 30 BC and AD 70), it's unlikely that Solomon had anything to do with it!

Tobit
Tobit tells the story of a Jew living in Nineveh. A devout, faithful blind man has his fortunes (and eyesight) restored through the actions of his son, Tobias, and the angel Raphael, disguised as a relative called Azariah. The book's message is that piety will be rewarded.

Judith
Judith is an Esther-like story of a Jewish woman living in Jerusalem when the city is under attack by the Assyrians. She sneaks into the enemy camp, seduces the Assyrian general, and cuts off his head, leading to an amazing victory. It was written by a Palestinian Jew with a very shaky grasp of history.

Others

As well as entire books, the Apocrypha also includes additions to existing books of the Old Testament.

- There are four extra parts of the book of Daniel. There are additions to the story of the young men in the fiery furnace (The Prayer of Azariah). The story of Susanna is perhaps the earliest detective story in the world and tells how Daniel rescues a woman unjustly accused of adultery. Bel and the Dragon (which becomes the Greek Daniel chapter 14) tells how Daniel escapes from a plot to put him to death.

- There are additions to the book of Esther, which include a new prologue, Mordecai's dream, letters from the emperor, and various prayers.

- The book of Baruch (who was Jeremiah's secretary) is an add-on to Jeremiah and contains a letter to the Jews in exile, as well as a prose prayer and two poems.

- The Prayer of Manasseh apparently relates the prayer of King Manasseh who, after a lifetime of wickedness, repents of his sins before he dies.

- Psalm 151 is an extra seven-verse psalm, celebrating David's defeat of Goliath.

The New Testament: Gospels and Acts

The New Testament falls into two main sections: the Gospels and Acts of the Apostles, and the letters.

Matthew

Matthew's Gospel has a very Jewish feel. It emphasizes the fulfilment of Old Testament prophecy, uses a lot of Jewish terminology, and contains more Old Testament quotes than any other Gospel. It aims to prove that Jesus is the messiah (so Matthew includes a family tree showing Jesus' descent from King David). But, although it is aimed at Jewish readers, Matthew's Gospel does not contain a narrow message. The kingdom is open to all, from whatever nation.

It contains much that is in the other synoptics – but also a lot of unique material. He gives us longer teaching from Jesus on the end times and different details about the supernatural events at the time of Jesus' resurrection. The emphasis is on "the kingdom of heaven". It ends with what is known as the great commission: Jesus' instruction to the disciples to go and spread the good news about him throughout the world.

Mark

This Gospel is the shortest of the four. The early church attributed it to John Mark, friend of Peter and Paul and relative of Barnabas (Acts 12:12; Colossians 4:10). Mark was probably writing mainly for a Gentile, Roman audience. He writes in a simple type of Greek, carefully explaining Jewish customs and translating Aramaic words and phrases.

He skips Jesus' birth, opening with his core message: "The beginning of the good news about

Jesus the Messiah, the Son of God." Mark's Jesus is
a healer, exorcist, and teacher, who is passionately
committed to the poor and the outcasts. The kingdom
of God is a place where the last are the first, where
leaders are slaves and servants. Mark's Gospel ends
abruptly, with no resurrection appearance – just two
women, an empty tomb, and an angel with a message
from God. Although some versions of Mark include
alternative, longer endings, these are later add-ons.
The original ending is probably lost.

Luke

Traditionally, this book has been attributed to Luke,
Paul's companion. He has prepared a carefully
researched account of Jesus for Theophilus (probably
a high-ranking Roman official). The result is not some
dry, stuffy history but a joyful, optimistic account.

In Luke's account, the poor and the marginalized
get the full blast of the good news. "He has brought
down rulers from their thrones but has lifted up the
humble," sings Mary, Jesus' mother. "He has filled the
hungry with good things but has sent the rich away
empty" (Luke 1:52–53). And that sums up the Gospel
of Luke. It's full of outsiders: tax collectors, prostitutes,
lepers, and thieves. The news of Jesus' birth comes
to humble, despised shepherds. There are Gentile
heroes as well: centurions and Samaritans. This is
the good news for all races. (Like Matthew, Luke
includes a genealogy, but his goes back to Adam, the
father of all.)

John

John's Gospel is very different from the other three: there is a different structure entirely. In the other Gospels Jesus is in Galilee and then goes up to Jerusalem. But in John's Gospel he makes at least four visits to Jerusalem. Similarly, there is more interpretation and reflection, not to mention some very long speeches. Although the Gospel is traditionally attributed to John, the author is never identified. He simply describes himself as "the disciple whom Jesus loved" (John 21:20).

From the start of John's Gospel, Jesus is much more than a human being; he is God, and always has been. As proof, Jesus performs seven miraculous signs, each telling us more about his nature and origins. And there are seven "I am…" statements, which tell us more about Jesus' nature. So this is more than a record of what Jesus did: it's a powerful, deep reflection on *who* he is.

Acts

The second part of Luke's two-part history of Christianity, Acts tells the story of the early church, from the resurrection of Jesus in Jerusalem to the imprisonment of Paul in Rome (around AD 62). (There are large chunks of the book where the writer uses the word "we", indicating that he was part of what was going on.) We see the young church finding its feet and spreading out from Jerusalem, through Judea, Samaria, and to other countries in the Roman empire.

The early Christians are empowered to do this by the Holy Spirit. Jesus promised his followers that he would send them the Holy Spirit, and in Acts the Spirit is a constant figure in the background, inspiring, protecting, informing, and pushing the first Christians to ever greater lengths as they spread the good news of Jesus Christ.

The New Testament: the letters

These fall into two groups. There are thirteen letters by Paul in the New Testament, although scholars argue as to whether all of them are really by Paul, or whether some are merely attributed to him. There are also letters by John, James, and Jude (Jesus' brothers) and Peter. Hebrews is anonymous and Revelation doesn't fit into any category!

Romans

Paul wrote this sometime in the spring of AD 57 to the church in Rome. He had never been there but he was planning a visit. However, this is more than an introductory note: it's packed with ideas about one of Paul's great theories – salvation by grace through faith. We are not saved because of what we do, but through faith in Jesus: this golden thread runs right through Romans. It is a powerful idea – a fundamental message of freedom – that has repeatedly fuelled reform and renewal of the church across the centuries. But this book is not all theory: the last four chapters of Romans are full of practical advice about how Christians are supposed to live Christ-shaped lives of love, peace, and hope.

1 and 2 Corinthians

These letters were written by Paul to the Christians in Corinth, an important, cosmopolitan city about 40 miles south-west of Athens. Paul had helped to establish the church in Corinth some three years earlier, but things have gone wrong. There is serious sexual sin in the church, not to mention schisms, arrogance, factionalism, and insincere worship. In 1 Corinthians, Paul calls on them to grow up and stop arguing. Above all, he talks about love. In one of the greatest pieces of prose ever written, he argues that love is the most important thing (1 Corinthians 13).

In between the first and the second letter Paul visited Corinth, but it was a painful trip. Eventually, though, he hears that his words have had some effect. The Corinthian church has changed its ways. In 2 Corinthians, Paul gives us a vivid impression of the cost of discipleship. He defends his apostleship by listing all that he has had to endure: imprisonment, beatings, shipwrecks, and unrelenting danger. But, Paul argues, God's grace is sufficient; his power is made perfect in weakness.

Galatians

Around AD 48–49 Paul made a journey into the Roman province of Galatia and founded churches there. Now, in an angry and entertainingly outspoken letter, he argues against those who claim that the Gentile converts he made in Galatia on his first journey must be circumcised and live as Jews. This is a passionate argument for freedom. The Galatians have been freed from slavery; now others want to enslave them to the Law. But Paul says it's no longer required. In one of the most radical statements in ancient history, Paul argues that there is no longer any difference between Jew and Gentile, slave and free, male and female: all are one in Jesus Christ (Galatians 3:26–29).

Ephesians

The letter brings together some of the major themes of Paul's teaching, as a kind of summary of his thoughts. Followers of Jesus need to recognize that we are all joined together and that we should all work for and support one another. No one is more important than another. Paul has an almost breathless tone of wonder at God's kindness, wisdom, and love. But he also talks about matter-of-fact things, such as controlling your tongue and your temper, and asking for God's protection against evil. It's been suggested that Ephesians was a letter to several churches: this would explain its general nature and the fact that it lacks any personal greetings.

Philippians

The church at Philippi had sent Paul a gift to support him while he was in prison (probably in Rome). Paul writes not only to thank them but also to warn them about possible pitfalls, and to encourage them to hold fast and keep going. The letter also contains one of the earliest statements of faith, a very early Christian hymn or poem, which summarizes early Christian belief about Jesus (Philippians 2:6–11).

Colossians

The Colossian church seems to have been lured into following a strange mash up of Jewish dietary laws, angel worship, and pagan new-moon festivals. Paul writes to encourage them to free themselves from such snares. The big message here is the supremacy of Christ. Christ is the true image of God, the ruler of all. He has disarmed all those powers, rulers, and authorities.

1 and 2 Thessalonians

Paul set up the church in Thessalonica around AD 50. In 1 Thessalonians he writes to address two main issues: when the Lord will return and what to do while waiting. Some of the Thessalonian believers have died before the Lord has returned. Paul says that they are not lost or gone. The Lord is coming again and the dead will rise first, and then we will all be with the Lord forever.

2 Thessalonians is a follow-up letter. The church in Thessalonica is still obsessing about the return of Jesus – some claim it has already happened and they have missed it – so Paul writes a further letter to give more information.

1 and 2 Timothy

1 Timothy is a manual for church leadership. Timothy
– whom Paul regards as a "son" – is now at Ephesus,
helping to lead the church there. Paul gives guidelines
on how to choose church leaders and combat false
teaching.

The second letter is very different. Paul is in prison
in Rome. He writes to ask Timothy to join him – and
also to encourage his protégé to persevere. Paul is
under no illusions: this could be the end. But he sees
the bigger picture. "If we died with him, we will also
live with him; if we endure, we will also reign with
him... " (2 Timothy 2:11–12). He urges Timothy to hold
on to sound teaching, to study the Scriptures, and to
keep on running the race.

Titus

Paul advises his co-worker Titus on leadership,
holiness, and honesty. This letter gives an insight
into the world of the early church and the qualities
required of their leaders. Church leaders should be
people of good reputation and personal behaviour.
Arguments and disputes should be avoided. But
upright lives are not just the work of leaders: all
Christians have a duty – young and old, slave and free.

Philemon

This is a request for reconciliation between a Christian
slave and his Christian master. There was a problem
between Onesimus and his boss. Some money or

expense seems to have been involved. Something has caused Philemon to believe that Onesimus was "useless" (Philemon 11). But Paul writes pleading that the two should be reconciled. Onesimus and Philemon are in the kingdom of God, where everyone is equal.

Hebrews

This is an interpretation of Jewish history and religious symbolism to show that Christ is the messiah. It was probably written to Jewish Christians in Rome. (Certainly it was written before the destruction of the Temple in Jerusalem in AD 70.) Hebrews argues that Christianity is the fulfilment of Judaism. The rules and regulations have been superseded, the barriers torn down. The unknown author scrolls through centuries of Jewish history, showing how its heroes have been characterized by faith. But even heroes such as Aaron, Moses, Abraham, and Joshua must bow to their superior, the one true high priest, Jesus Christ.

James

This letter is about putting faith into action. It was written by the brother of Jesus and leader of the Jerusalem church, although, with true humility, he describes himself simply as a servant of God and of the Lord Jesus Christ. James (his real name was Jacob) writes that faith has to be lived out. He champions the rights of the poor, criticizes snobs and bigots, and urges us to control our tongues. This emphasis on actions has led some to accuse James of not being

"Christian" enough. But this letter actually contains more quotes from Christ than all the other New Testament letters put together.

1 and 2 Peter

These letters are attributed to Peter, the apostle and friend of Jesus. 1 Peter is a circular letter to Christian Jews living in the Greco-Roman world. They are being marginalized and persecuted, and Peter writes to strengthen and encourage them.

2 Peter was written to combat false teaching. People are taking the words of others – for example, Paul's letters – and twisting them to suit their own ends. Some even deny that Jesus is coming, but Peter argues that God's timetable is not the same as ours.

1 John

John is writing to combat false teaching. Some people are promising secret knowledge to their "initiates". John tells his readers how they can be sure of their status as children of God and how the only test of true Christianity is whether the people demonstrate the love of Christ.

2 and 3 John

John writes about some leaders who have caused a split in the Christian community. In 2 John he encourages the followers to avoid false teachers. In 3

John he writes to a follower called Gaius, promising that he will come to sort out the split caused by a troublemaker named Diotrephes.

Jude

The book is attributed to Jude (or Judas), brother of James and Jesus (Matthew 13:55; Mark 6:3). He encourages believers to stay strong in the faith and to reject false teaching and failing leadership. Jude wanted to write a different letter, but has changed tack because certain "intruders" have infiltrated the church: people who pervert the grace of God.

Revelation

Revelation is an astonishing, vivid, epic, anti-imperial, apocalyptic tract. John is a prisoner on an island, when he sees a vision. A figure "like a son of man" (1:13), gives John messages addressed to the "angels" (1:20) of seven churches in the Roman province of Asia (modern western Turkey). After this John is shown a series of apocalyptic images, culminating in the final creation of a new heaven and a new earth where God will live in harmony with all his people. It was written at a time when churches were facing persecution by Rome, the great imperial power. But the message of Revelation is that Christ is triumphant, not the powers of the world. Whoever is in charge at the moment, whichever petty worldly power thinks it has the victory, is mistaken; in the end, God wins.

6. How do we read the Bible?

If you've made it this far you'll have a reasonable idea of what the Bible contains, the story it tells, the way it's all organized, and even how it came to be compiled.

Maybe by now you feel like you want to read it for yourself. Despite the title of this book, the Bible is not a book for experts. Of course, experts will help us in exploring the text, understanding it, and applying it, but the Bible is not just for them. It's intended for everyone.

So I'd really encourage you to try reading it for yourself. And here – in appropriately biblical fashion – are my ten commandments for reading the Bible.

1. Get a good translation

Many people have an old copy of the Bible in the house or a family Bible, which is almost certain to be the King James Version. Now the KJV has many strengths but it's not exactly user-friendly. If you want to read the Bible for yourself, I would really recommend getting hold of a modern, accessible translation.

Some Modern Versions
Some of the most accessible versions are:

• Contemporary English Version (CEV)

• New International Version (NIV)

• New Living Translation (NLT)

• Good News Bible (GNB)

• English Standard Version (ESV)

• New Revised Standard Version (NRSV)

• The Message.

The best thing to do is to go into a bookshop with a range of Bibles – a Christian bookshop should have such a range – and have a look. Or you can easily find most versions on the web. So you can try them out for yourself.

2. Take your time

Read slowly and carefully. Some of the problems we encounter in reading the Bible come about because we rush. The Bible wasn't built for speed reading. As we've seen, for most of its history the Bible has been more of an audiobook – read aloud to people. So it also helps to read it aloud, and that slows you down as well.

3. See the bigger picture

It helps to read in fairly large chunks. Read a chapter, rather than a handful of verses. Read the whole psalm, rather than just one line. With parts of the Gospels, for example, it helps to see the events "either side" of the passage you might be reading. Often a parable might have some specific connection with the place or time in which it is being told. This will enable you to see the context, which can be really helpful in understanding that particular section.

4. Ask questions

This is, in a way, the most important tool in reading the Bible (or any great text for that matter): always ask questions. Who is saying this? Why is this happening? When is this story set? Who is this guy? What does that mean? List the questions and then use the tools below to find out the answers. Some people find it helpful to make notes as they go along. You can draw diagrams, pictures, and maps. You can write down the questions you need to explore. Some people keep special notebooks for this purpose; others write in the margins of their Bibles.

5. Get some help

As we've seen, the Bible was written in different languages, a long time ago. While a lot of it is straightforward, some parts are very deep and complex. In those cases it's a good thing to get some expert help.

Here are a few tools that will help you if you really want to understand the Bible.

- **A study Bible:** This is a Bible that comes with notes and articles, maps, and other resources. Different study Bibles have different emphases – some of them aim to help you understand the history and culture, while others focus on particular types of readers or applications.

- **A Bible atlas:** This is a useful tool for understanding the geography and setting of the Bible. One of my favourites is *The One Stop Bible Atlas*, written by... er... me. Others, of course, are available.

- **A Bible dictionary:** This is an A–Z of Bible topics, people, ideas, themes, and so on. You can get good one-volume ones.

- **A Bible handbook:** The classic is *The Lion Handbook to the Bible*, first published in 1973 and still going strong. (I've done one of these as well, but modesty forbids...)

- **Commentaries:** If you want to take things further and go deeper into a particular book, then a commentary might help. These are books that offer an in-depth study of an individual Bible book. Some of them are very academic, but there are plenty that are more popular in style.

6. Work out what type of writing it is

As we have seen, the Bible is a mix of different types of writing, including poetry and prose, lists, laws, stories, and proverbs. These things have to be read differently. So always ask yourself, "What type of writing is this?" This will help in understanding a passage.

7. Explore the history and culture

Some of your questions will only be answered by understanding the historical setting. In the story of the Good Samaritan, for example, it's crucial to the understanding of the story to know a bit about why Jews and Samaritans hated each other. Where a place is mentioned it sometimes helps to locate it on a map. This is where those background tools come in. A good study Bible, Bible guide, or commentary will really help in giving you the background on the times and customs of the Old and New Testament.

8. Work to a plan

Sometimes it helps to have a plan of action. Maybe you want to read through one book of the Bible. Maybe you want to find out about one particular person or place, or explore what the Bible has to say about a topic. There are plenty of reading plans available to help you. Some Bibles have reading plans in them, or you can find them on the internet, or from organizations such as the Bible Reading Fellowship or Scripture Union.

9. Use your common sense

The Bible is big on the concept of wisdom. So we should take notice of that. Don't go flying off into wild theories or flights of imagination that are not supported by the text. By all means come up with your own ideas about a passage, but check them out with some of the expert tools.

10. Don't worry if you don't understand it all

Here's a secret: nobody understands *all* of the Bible. There are parts of the Bible that are so old or obscure that they reduce even the greatest experts to shoulder-shrugging and scratching of heads. For example, thirty-nine psalms end with the word "*selah*" but no one knows what this means for sure.

Even where we know what all the individual words mean, there are confusing passages and theological ideas on which there are many different opinions. So you will never fully understand the Bible. The thing is not to worry too much about that. Instead, we should concentrate on what we *do* understand. There are plenty of complex parts of the Bible, but a great many more where the meaning is straightforward.

7. The strange country

The great theologian Karl Barth once attempted to describe what was different about the Bible: "What is there within the Bible? What sort of house is it to which the Bible is the door? What sort of country is spread before our eyes when we throw the Bible open?"

Barth went on to talk about "the strange new world within the Bible". In a way I think this is the best possible description of this indescribable book. Yes, the Bible is a collection of books. But it is more than that: it is – whatever our beliefs – a fascinating, wonderful, strange world to explore.

And the amazing thing is that, Tardis-like, the Bible is so much bigger on the inside. In the strange new world of the Bible, no matter how much you know about it, there is always more to discover.

So crack open the covers of that book. Enter the land. Start exploring.

The journey begins here.